Born For A Purpose

Born For A Purpose

Ruth Weller

All rights reserved

No part of this book may be reproduced in any form without written permission from the author

Ruth Weller, Tarn Hows, Woburn Lane, Aspley Guise, Milton Keynes, MK17 8JN

Acknowledgements

My thanks go to the people who have helped me to write this small book, "Born For a Purpose."

They include my patient husband, John, who used his computer skills to transpose my handwritten script into one that was legible. To my English teacher from my school days, Wendy Godfrey, who worked so thoroughly with my original script. I value the support and prayers I have received, especially from Mary Hammond and Liz Macey.

Finally I would like to thank the Community at Willen Priory, Milton Keynes, for providing a serene atmosphere wherein I could write my book.

Ruth Weller
September 1995

In memory of
John and Dorothy Ducker
who gave us love and support

Contents

		Page
	Preface	3
1	Preparation for Rachel	5
2	The Birth	7
3	Is She to Die?	10
4	The Aftermath	13
5	Integration with Peer Group	16
6	Rachel Shares God's Love	19
7	The Move	21
8	We Change Denominations	23
9	Confirmation Preparation Begins	26
10	Sharing a Meal with Jesus	28
11	The Confirmation and After	30
12	The Miracle is Broken	32
13	Gethsemane	35
14	Reality	38
15	Rachel's Ministry	41
16	Conclusion	43

Preface

I wanted to write this book because of the love our Down's Syndrome daughter, Rachel, has generated within our own family and with the people she has met.

Her gentleness, her outstretched arms waiting to enfold you in a hug, have been part of her personality since she was a young child. Her communication is through love as she has little language.

Alongside her love is a deep sensitivity, an awareness of people's feelings. If people are afraid of her or, worse still, reject her, she withdraws like a snail into her shell. I then feel sad because that rejection, that fear, becomes a barrier and Rachel's love cannot be received.

Is this similar to our relationship with God? When we set up barriers between ourselves and God, are we then not open to receive His love?

This is one of the few ways that Rachel through her love, through her personality, has led me into a deeper understanding of God's love for us.

Rachel and people who are similar to her are people of worth; not to be despised or rejected. My prayer is that, as you read this book, it will not only give you a deeper understanding of people with a mental handicap, but that you will be brought closer to God.

I feel so strongly that Rachel was born for a purpose.

Chapter 1

Preparation for Rachel

When I was twenty three years old, I went to the Keswick Convention. There I bought a book called "Angel Unawares" by Roy Roger's wife, Dale Evans. The book describes their daughter's ministry. Robin had only lived for two years, deformed physically and mentally. Surely, it would have been better if she had died at birth? As I began to read through the book, my attitude began to change. This child in her simplicity had drawn people into so much prayer, so much pain and so much joy.

I was then a teacher of young children and I 'stored' the contents of this book within my mind, at the same time developing a subtle interest in handicapped children.

Two years later I was appointed to a post as a teacher of partially sighted children. Within this small group of eleven children there was a broad spectrum of abilities, behaviour patterns and handicaps. Through trial and error I learnt to meet the children where they each were and not where I thought they ought to be!

In 1966 I moved to Surrey when I married John. I applied to an ordinary State school for a teaching post, I was not successful as I made a mess of the interview. A week later I was invited to another school for children with moderate learning difficulties. I was chosen for the post from a number of applicants.

At St. Philip's School I taught children from seven years old to teenagers - a challenging job meeting challenging behaviour, children deprived of love and children deprived of a good brain. I had to be cautious about not becoming too involved with individual children. Once more I found that I had to meet each child where he or she was and not where I felt they ought to be. It was hard work but fun, with groups of twenty children.

After two years of marriage, John and I felt that we wanted to start a family. Andrew was born in August 1969 followed by Martin in 1972. John and I revelled in their childhood, trying our best to give them positive emotional, physical and spiritual foundations. We had the joy of watching two very different personalities develop.

But we wanted a daughter. When Andrew was five and Martin two years old I became pregnant once more. Was it going to be Sebastian or Imogen? I fantasised about Imogen: the clothes she would wear, a bedroom white and pink, filled with dolls. Would I have the sensitivity to create an open mother and daughter relationship in the teenage years? My head was full of these thoughts when I went into labour in the early hours of Maundy Thursday 1975.

At 6.40 a.m. I gave birth to a daughter. For the first seven hours of her life I reflected with great joy on my expectations, so happy. However by 1.50 p.m., Imogen and all my expectations were no longer reality.

Later I would mourn her loss. A loss that would remain alive within our daughter, Rachel Suzanna.

~~~~~ ◊ ~~~~~

Chapter 2

The Birth

John and I were very fortunate that we had been able to choose a hospital administered by a Roman Catholic Order for the births of Martin and Rachel.

Following Rachel's birth, I was placed in a private room; I was assured that it wouldn't cost us any extra money, but it would enable me to rest. I couldn't understand why I hadn't been able to nurse our daughter as soon as she was born. In my naivete I thought that the nuns were too busy first thing in the morning and they were anxious that I should receive my rest. The morning wore on. People popped in and out of my room. I tried to tell them excitedly about my daughter, how I was going to decorate her room, my joy complete. But no-one stopped to listen! It was snowing outside - a white Easter! Oh well, never mind, John would enjoy taking the boys out sledging. The morning became afternoon. I was hungry, where was my daughter? I wanted to see her. I put the radio on. It was "The Archers", where was everybody?

There was a knock on my door and in came the doctor who had delivered our baby daughter. He was the husband of my G.P. My first words to him were the fact that I was hungry. Did he know where my lunch was? I am afraid he ignored my question. I noticed that he looked apprehensive. I became puzzled when he began talking about my career as a teacher of handicapped children and the fact that that experience would now come in useful. He then went on to say that our daughter was a 'mongol' or in modern terminology, had Downs Syndrome.

My initial reaction to the doctor must have been one of relief as I replied that I would accept her as a challenge, because racing through my mind was all the preparation that God had given me over the past twelve years for this baby's birth. It fitted together like a jigsaw. I wanted to see her.

The door opened and the nun who had helped me with the delivery came in with a baby in her arms. She presented me with Rachel Suzanna saying to me: "This child has been born for a purpose". I looked at Rachel who looked so chubby and content. I said to her, "You cannot help it. We will love you just the same as though you were a normal child". Then I turned to the nun and pleaded for my dinner! Despite everything my hunger was paramount! My dinner arrived and Rachel was placed in a small cot by my bed.

As I ate I thought of my family. Did John know? Did the boys know? How would my elderly parents react? They knew how much I wanted a daughter.

Soon the nun popped her head around the door and announced that I had a visitor. The Rev. John Ducker our wonderful minister from the little Methodist church the children and I went to in our village.

He opened his arms and gave me a hug, then he sat by my bed and held my hand. We cried and we prayed, we cried and we prayed for about two hours. In the midst of this he assured me that John knew. He and the boys would soon be coming in to see us. John had spoken on the telephone to our minister, who had rushed to the hospital to see me, but the nuns had asked if he could return later as soon as the Doctor had given me the news.

I felt enfolded by love and this gave me the strength to cope.

Later, early in the evening, John came in with Andrew and Martin. We all nursed Rachel. John told me how he and the doctor had looked at Rachel in a crib soon after her birth. They had discussed Rachel's condition and the doctor wanted affirmation from a Paediatrician before confronting me.

We just huddled together that evening, nursing Rachel. We were a family unit, perhaps afraid of the future, but grateful at that moment in time for the privacy of a single room.

Next day, Good Friday, our G.P. a mother of three children wanted to see John and me together. How we valued those two hours she spent with us. It was wisdom she gave us not sentimentality. She talked of Andrew and Martin, that in no way must they be neglected because of the attention we would need to give to Rachel. We saw the advantage of having two sons and suggestions were given to John of how his father's rôle would need to be very strong with them, giving me more time to concentrate on Rachel.

Our sons somehow became more precious to us during this time. Rachel fed well and appeared healthy. Our doctor encouraged us to be proud of her and "show her off". People would respond positively to this attitude and it would lessen rejection. Our doctor stayed with me after John left and remarked how fortunate I was to have a husband like John, who had accepted Rachel and was being very supportive. She admired his maturity. Was he too part of God's plan, part of the wonderful way He had prepared us for Rachel?

I stayed in the hospital for a week. Friends from our small church were so supportive. They visited me, fed John and the children. Our minister came every day to see us. On Easter Monday, Rachel received both a Methodist Blessing and a Catholic Blessing. My G.P. came frequently too and the nuns bestowed on us their love and nursing care.

Within this environment our little family was given the strength, the support and encouragement to cope with the future. During that week we learned to love Rachel dearly.

When she was a week old, we took her home, ready to face the ordinary world. Would our faith and trust in God survive?

Chapter 3

Is She to Die?

The snow had disappeared and it was the abundance of daffodils in our garden that welcomed Rachel and me to our home in West Horsley. We took her upstairs to a bedroom we had prepared for her nursery and laid her in a beautiful crib lent to me by our dear friend, Pam.

Rachel appeared content and soon went off to sleep. I then realised that she could still have a pretty decorated room, I could still dress her in attractive dresses. Rachel's handicap need not deprive me of those delights.

For the first few weeks someone came and helped me with the housework, John went back to work, Andrew went back to school, Martin, Rachel and I began to settle down to some kind of routine. Rachel was an easy baby, fed slowly but slept well.

She was soon accepted in our village and church community. People were so kind and we were inundated with pretty dresses and frilly pants for her. I found the first pram trip down to our village hard - behind me I saw my friend pushing her new born baby, Elizabeth, who was perfect. There was a lump in my throat, but we battled on. The next time, Martin sat in a new elevated position on top of the pram - fun! We ventured forth with smiles on our faces. People stopped us and we showed them Rachel. We were proud of her. This was the beginning of our long walks to the shops. The distance remained the same, but people would always stop us, tell us their stories of disappointment or of friends they knew who had handicapped children.

At six weeks Rachel smiled at us. She was level with her peers! More important, she was level with Dr. Spock's theories of Child Development! Had the doctors made an incorrect diagnosis? Was she normal after all? My elderly parents travelled down to see us. Rachel was so responsive. Surely, they thought, a mistake had been made.

This jubilation didn't last for very long. When Rachel was eight weeks old our health visitor came with the result of Rachel's blood test definitely testifying that Rachel had Down's Syndrome.

She was going to be the best Down's Syndrome child that ever lived!! In my determination I sang to her, I massaged her legs, I put her in a bouncing cradle chair to sit and watch the boys. I was glad that she was bottle fed as I soon found myself exhausted. John was able to give her the night feed. He didn't feel rejected by the situation, and a bond began to grow between him and Rachel.

We made new friends after being introduced to the local society for the Mentally Handicapped. Our small Methodist church continued to support us as a family and life because of Rachel seemed more enriched.

Regular check-ups on Rachel were made at our local County Hospital. In June a heart murmur was discovered. We were told that Rachel would need to have various tests. We were assured that this was quite common in Down's children. We tried not to worry, but no-one seemed anxious to give us the results of her tests. We had a family holiday at Margate in August and felt a normal happy family. However, on our return, we were told that Rachel had a hole in her heart and that nothing could be done.

Two days before her christening I felt devastated. I could do something with her lack of intelligence through stimulation, but not with her heart. There was nothing I could do but give her to God.

Colds and bronchitis became the pattern that winter. No longer did Rachel put on any weight. Numerous antibiotics were prescribed for her. Surely God hadn't meant this? But did He? On the eleventh of December 1975, Rachel was admitted to hospital with double pneumonia. On the eighteenth of December, Rachel went into heart failure; she wasn't responding to treatment. To our horror there was a suggestion made to us that treatment should be withdrawn and she should be made comfortable! No, no, no, no! Our trust in humanity left us: only our trust in God remained.

Our neighbours were kind and looked after Andrew and Martin for us. How I valued their support! On Friday the twenty first of December I arrived at the hospital to find Rachel had had her second heart failure. She recovered only to have another a few hours later.

I had written all our Christmas cards the previous evening and had asked our friends to pray, but would the cards get there in time? We were told that there wasn't any hope. I couldn't reach Rachel. She was swathed in an oxygen tent. I was desperate to touch her. I felt I could pass on some strength to her if I did that. I managed to glide my hand under the plastic sheeting and before long I was able to touch her hand. Oh God, please help! Don't let Rachel die!

John and I were advised to go home and rest. We would need our energy next day. Before we went to bed, we telephoned as many of our friends as we could and asked for their prayers. I just lay awake that night dreading the 'phone would ring.

Saturday morning came - no news. I dare not, I dare not telephone the hospital. John was concerned about our sons. To lighten the situation they decorated the house ready for Christmas. The telephone rang - I couldn't answer it - was it bad news? No, it was John Ducker our minister enquiring how she was. We plucked up courage - we telephoned the hospital. Rachel was still alive!

We all drove to the hospital to be told that Rachel seemed to be responding to treatment, that a change had happened overnight.

Later that day a nurse told us that she had seen our minister, John Ducker, praying with Rachel. The nurse thought it was because Rachel had died, but that had been her turning point. Ten days later we brought Rachel home.

~~~~~ ◊ ~~~~~

Chapter 4

The Aftermath

The week after Christmas 1975 was the first of many when we felt socially isolated. We knew people were supporting us with prayer. Rachel was getting better. We knew people were meeting our physical needs. Casseroles and cakes were frequently left on our door step. But what about our emotional needs? No-one knocked on our door and during that week the telephone was silent. Were people afraid that Rachel had died? Were they frightened of facing our tears? Most likely they were celebrating Christmas with family and friends. Life must go on. On New Year's Day we brought Rachel home and soon the school next door to our house was filled with children returning after their Christmas Break. I needed a sign to tell people that Rachel was home, Rachel was well. I was tearful though. Would people be able to cope with tears? Despite it being winter, I put nappies, plastic pants and bibs on the washing line where people would see them. Gradually people began to pluck up courage and knock at our door; friends who had received our Christmas cards began to telephone. The latter I couldn't cope with - I cried, so John took the calls. However, we began to feel strengthened by this outward show of people's love.

The weather was kind to us that winter. John and I invested in a sturdy pushchair which would enable Rachel to sit up and this would help her breathing. On my Mother's advice I took Rachel for a daily walk with Martin walking by our side. Rachel's cheeks bloomed, but sadly Martin caught the flu.

Life continued with Rachel's health going up and down. I was determined that she would not return to hospital. Many hours were spent patting her back to empty the fluid from her lungs. Her in built thermostat didn't operate very well, so we had to keep all our rooms at an even temperature I had to adapt her clothes when we went in and out of shops. Sometimes - once for as long as five weeks - Rachel was so ill that we couldn't take her out. At times like this I really felt trapped in a prison and outwardly there were signs that I was worn out.

However there were many blessings. Had we been led to buy this spacious semi - detached house next door to a combined Lower and Middle School? It meant there was no need, when Rachel was ill, for me to take Andrew to school. The previous owners had built onto our garage a large extension, which we turned into a playroom. The boys could play with their friends here, without too much supervision from me. We lived within easy reach of London; many a week-end John would take the boys there to see the sights and enjoy the museums. We had held onto our doctor's advice not to neglect our sons. How grateful I was to John and our situation that enabled them to develop according to their potential even though I had to concentrate on Rachel.

Thanks be to God.

Gradually Rachel began to improve. The bouts of bronchitis became less and physically she began to develop slowly in her own time. At two years old she was pushing a trolley of bricks and then a doll's pram around the Crescent where we lived. To our delight, at two years ten months she walked on her own!

It still took us a long time to walk to our village with Rachel in her pushchair. People stopped to enquire kindly about Rachel. One lady, Mae, who rarely went to church, told me that she prayed for Rachel every day. Other people told me this too - Rachel became known as "The Little Girl we pray for". But she was better. Why were people praying? Then I learnt that stories were circulating about children with heart conditions similar to Rachel's being healed, the holes automatically closing. Could this happen to Rachel? This is what people were praying for. I enquired from the medical profession if this would be a possibility with Rachel? No, I was told, it rarely happens to children with Down's Syndrome.

Just before Rachel's third birthday she went for a medical check up, which took place every six months. I remember she wouldn't walk for the doctor, but crawled around the room, the doctor plus stethoscope crawling after her. No murmur from Rachel's heart could be heard! Further tests showed that the hole in Rachel's heart had been healed.

A miracle.

~~~~~ ◊ ~~~~~

Chapter 5

Integration with Peer Group

The photograph on the cover of this book was taken soon after we were told that Rachel's hole in her heart had closed. The look of joy on her face reflects our feelings. Now I felt that I could do something positive with her to develop her intelligence. Martin was now at school so I had more time just for Rachel.

John and I had been introduced to the Downs Association. Twice each year they had meetings not far from us in Cheam.

Those meetings were packed with parents similar to ourselves, who were determined to learn how they could provide a better quality of life for their Down's children. We were inspired and encouraged to demand the best from professionals. Our children were children first, who happened to have a handicap. At those meetings we learnt the importance of our children playing with and being stimulated by normal children. Integration of our Downs children into normal playgroups, nursery schools and ordinary schools was paramount. This situation is something we had to fight for!

Encouraged by what we heard at these meetings, John and I began to work out how we could integrate Rachel with her peers. Because I had taught handicapped children, no-one in authority persuaded us that Rachel should go to a school for children with severe learning difficulties, not until she was five years old.

We had a small crêche and Sunday School at our Methodist Church, and from a babyhood Rachel was automatically accepted into these groups. Our minister's wife, Dorothy, led an excellent Playgroup, which our sons had attended. Dorothy put Rachel's name down as soon as she was born. Rachel was just three years old when she started this group, soon to be joined by Elizabeth, my friend's baby daughter mentioned in an earlier chapter. At one year old, Elizabeth had been diagnosed as partially deaf. Dorothy was only too happy to welcome our children who happened to have a handicap into her stimulating Playgroup. Rachel and Elizabeth were so happy in that environment.

Rachel attended two days each week. I began to think of our assets, the large room attached to our garage, my qualifications as a nursery/infant teacher, our proximity to the local school and the fact that there were approximately six other children living in our Crescent who were of a similar age to Rachel. I began to wonder if I could run a small Nursery Group within our home. The idea developed, so one day each week five children met with Rachel in our home for two hours. There was no charge, but there was a rota for mothers to take it in turn each week to help me and to provide the materials for a specific activity and the refreshments. For just over two years this happy group met every Wednesday in term time. Rachel was really integrated within it. The two hours were structured: creative activities and music, a break, free play and a story to end. We had parties and outings, but above all fun. Rachel was part of the community and not isolated from it.

However, despite all this integration with her peer group, speech was not developing, although she was socially very acceptable.

Alongside the Playgroup and my own Nursery Group I decided to do five minutes structured teaching with her each day. I began by putting a few favourite toys in front of her and asking her to show me for example - a ball. As she learnt to do this, I progressed to toy animals, colours and everyday objects. Only occasionally was she was able to name the object, but at least she had comprehension. We moved on to Lotto games. I made books where she could match pictures. At four years old she was beginning to match letter to post box, needle to thread and sort objects into groups. She could hold a pencil, trace a line, go over her written name and recognise her name when it was mixed with others.

These skills developed into her being able to draw a face, recognise a few sounds phonetically and say them! What a joy that was! How I enjoyed these years. Rachel was pure delight to be with and to teach.

I remember one incident when she had watched me crack eggs into a basin. The following Wednesday she found half a dozen eggs left by a farmer's wife on our back door step. She picked them up, found what she thought was a bowl and cracked the eggs into it. Unfortunately the bowl was a colander!

We did have fun!

At five years old we were told that there would be no alternative but send her to a School for Children with Severe Learning difficulties, on a daily basis, ten miles away from our home.

Rachel still had very little language and control of her waterworks wasn't brilliant. Would these factors be of paramount importance to the staff at her new school? If so, would they see beyond these disabilities and relate to our happy, sociable daughter?

It was with these concerns in my mind that I hugged my daughter as I left her in the classroom of her new school, one morning in April 1980.

Rachel didn't settle. I was frequently in tears during the next six months. A very precious part of my life with Rachel had come to an end.

Chapter 6

Rachel Shares God's Love

If Rachel had difficulty communicating with the spoken word, she didn't have any difficulty communicating with her outward show of affection. As she grew older I began to observe an inner sensitivity to people in pain.

Her birth was surrounded with love and because she was a placid baby people were keen to hold her in their arms. Andrew and Martin enjoyed playing with her. From a babyhood she was given and radiated out so much love.

Her first missionary experience was at the age of three months. The nuns from the Nursing Home, where she was born, asked me to visit a mother and her newly born Down's syndrome son in their maternity unit. Rachel greeted the mother with smiles.

Rachel's illnesses drew prayer from people who rarely went to church. The healing of her heart encouraged people to pray more - their prayers had been answered.

I was a pastoral visitor in our Methodist church. I soon realised how much easier it was to relate to people if Rachel was with me. Shy people focused on her, she wasn't threatening, they could relate to me through her. One dear friend from my childhood, at the age of eighty, became almost like a skeleton through cancer. When Rachel and I visited her, Rachel gently took the old lady's head into her arms, stroked her wispy hair and kissed her. That old lady's face shone. She had received love, God's love through Rachel?

I too had to learn to communicate through love. From being a small child I had been so shy of giving any outward show of affection and withdrew from anyone who dare offer me a kiss. God must have known how much I needed to learn how to love. Rachel has taught me so much. As a result we have a very loving relationship within our family; we are not frightened of hugs and kisses. But it is only in recent years that I have had the courage to give any outward show of affection towards people beyond our immediate family. Rachel has shown me the importance of touch, of holding hands to bring comfort and healing, and just to open my arms to people in pain and give them a big hug.

A smile, a smile of love can do so much to bring Gods's joy into a situation of apprehension and fear.

When Rachel was ten years old I had the privilege of going into an Old People's Home to help with a monthly service of Holy Communion. In between these services John, Rachel and I would visit them on a Sunday. Many of the residents' minds and memories had gone - but Rachel didn't know that. Each one of them would hold Rachel's hand, smile at her, relate to her and then relate to John and me, Rachel kissed them - so I kissed them, Rachel hugged them, so I plucked up courage to hug them. We sang hymns together, those they could remember from their Sunday School days. I remember this time as a very precious ministry, which John, Rachel and I did together.

And Rachel's ministry to me? I can only describe this within a poem.

> Together we sit.
> Rachel and I
> In the Lady Chapel,
> Safe and still.
> Slowly, in my imagination,
> My child within
> Becomes my child without.
> She sits upon my knee,
> And I nurse her sensitive scars
> Which were once deep wounds,
> Tears trickling down my face.
> Gently, Rachel with her great capacity to love
> Enfolds us both in her arms.

~~~~~ ◊ ~~~~~

Rachel with her family, 1991

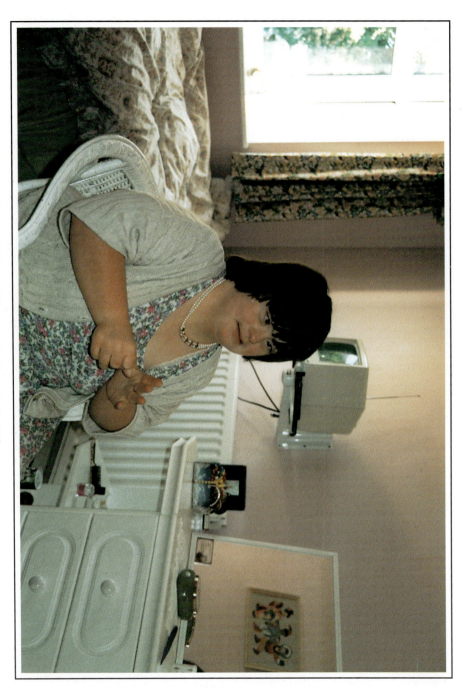

Rachel, aged 20 years, in her bed-sitting room

Chapter 7

The Move

1984 saw a big change in the circumstances of the Weller Family. John's office was moving out of central London to the city of the concrete cows - Milton Keynes! How we fought against that move. We were so happy in our village of Horsley, our two sons were settled into school and Andrew was due to take nine subjects at "O" level in 1985.

However Milton Keynes wasn't all "Lego Land" and concrete cows! Travelling was easy and the shops were wonderful.

We found a beautiful village on the outskirts of Milton Keynes, in Bedfordshire and a good school for Andrew and Martin. The staff at the school were very co-operative at addressing their needs, giving Andrew their time because of the pressure of "O" levels the following year. Our new home was built on a hill commanding wonderful views and there was a large garden to maintain.

Just after her ninth birthday, Rachel started at her new school in Bedford. To our amazement she soon settled. The water works problem, which had plagued her, her teachers and ourselves for four years previously, stopped within a week of her starting her new school.

Had God planned this for us? Was it to stir us out of our complacency? Was it to give our children greater opportunities? How could Rachel continue her mission, in Aspley Guise of sharing God's love with the people she met?

During the first six months after our move, God and I had a lot of conversations together! I missed the community of our little Methodist church and the community of the village in Surrey where Rachel had been the "The Little Girl We Pray For".

I visited several churches of various denominations in and around Aspley Guise, sometimes with John, sometimes with Rachel, sometimes alone. Rachel could say "Amen" in a loud voice, accepted in our small Methodist church, but not in the middle of a sermon or prayers in a strange church. People were kind to us but I couldn't find God "At Home", where I could be at ease with Rachel.

We tried our local church in the village. There were so many robed people. The choir and a few other people processed around the church. They used a prayer book, which despite my Anglican upbringing, I had never seen before. But above all at every Sunday Morning service, Holy Communion was celebrated. How could we worship here? Rachel said "Amen" in the wrong places, especially when everybody was quiet and solemn, and how could John participate in the Service? He hadn't been christened, let alone confirmed. Was there a suitable group for Andrew and Martin? Oh, how I longed to be back at our Methodist church at West Horsley! My faith was important to me, a church family was important to me, I wanted John and Rachel to be accepted and respected.

I wrestled with this problem for six months. A beautiful house but how lonely I was! I plucked up courage after three months and took Rachel to an evening service at the local Anglican Church. It was to be "Songs of Praise"; perhaps it wouldn't matter if Rachel made a noise. People were kind and welcomed both of us. Rachel participated in the singing.

The Friday afterwards, in the evening, the Rector visited us in our house. We shared our problems and we prayed. His parting words to us were, "Let us see what we can do together".

~~~~~ ◊ ~~~~~

Chapter 8

We Change Denominations

"Let us see what we can do together". I kept on churning these words over in my mind as a cow chews the cud.

As a result, I went along to the Sunday Morning Parish Communion, acquainted myself with the 'Alternative Service Book' and began to value the receiving at Communion each week. The Rector's sermons were excellent. They were about love not sin - God loved me, but above all I was to love myself because God had created me! Having received the outward love from Rachel, I revelled in this new teaching for me. Repentance and sin were replaced by God's love and I was thirsty for it.

John attended various evening services but was hesitant to come to the Morning Communion Service, so how could I take Rachel? She couldn't disturb these wonderful sermons!

I continued to cry - "Lord where can I take Rachel?" In the September, one Saturday afternoon, I was crying with despair in the utility room, when I heard a leaflet drop through our letter box. I picked it up and read the words "Children are welcome in church. Here are various ideas on how to keep them quiet".

"Thank you God", I thought, this is my affirmation that we should attend our local Anglican Church in Aspley Guise, address our problems and trust in God.

John soon found out that he could receive a Blessing during communion and I took Rachel into the vestry during the sermon where a group of younger children were having their Sunday School. Sadly it meant my missing our Rector's excellent sermons, but I felt it was important that John should receive teaching. I could attend a bible study led by our Rector and receive teaching there.

It was different. I still missed the community of our Methodist Church, but the teaching I was receiving and my experiencing God's presence and peace at the celebration of Holy Communion, was bringing me so close to God and giving me a totally new experience of God's Love. For the first time in my life I began to value myself.

John had begun going to our Methodist Church after Rachel was born, he valued the members' support, but here he could relate to our Rector's teaching. They could talk and explore in an academic way. One year after our move to Aspley Guise he joined three other men for a confirmation class.

On October 13th 1985, John was christened and confirmed by Bishop David of Bedford. Was Rachel born for this purpose?

Sadly Andrew and Martin, then into teenage years, were not interested in church. However their relationship with Rachel was one of protection and love. Some of these qualities flowed into their relationships with John, myself and their friends.

During the following two years we became more involved within the Church Family. I became a Sunday School teacher, taking Rachel with me as a helper; I also became a Baptismal Pastoral Visitor and Rachel came with me visiting various homes. Once more I found that people had the courage to be quite open with me, because Rachel in her simplicity created a non-threatening atmosphere.

John was receiving a peace and was also feeling a presence of God through the celebration of Holy Communion. Would it be possible for Rachel to receive this peace? Would she be able to be confirmed? When she was twelve, a chaplain from a Residential Home for people with special needs, mentioned to us that it would be possible. The chaplain kindly mentioned the possibility to our Rector. We had a short discussion, but decided to put it on hold for at least one year.

Meanwhile, John, Rachel and I had become members of an Anglican "Faith & Light Community". This movement had been initiated by a priest, Jean Vanier in France, who had found God within people with special needs. The "Faith & Light" Communities are for families which include a member with a disability. The Communities meet on a regular basis to celebrate together, share a meal and to worship God. John and I shared with the members of this community the possibility of Rachel being confirmed. We were encouraged and supported by them.

In April 1988 just after Rachel's thirteenth birthday, I asked our Rector if Rachel could be confirmed alongside her peer group in the following November.

Chapter 9

Confirmation Preparation Begins

We decided to prepare Rachel for confirmation. Permission was granted from Bishop John of St. Albans.

But how should we prepare? Rachel had very little language and limited comprehension. The Rector decided that it wouldn't be any use her going to the Confirmation Class with her peers.

Rachel would only be able to concentrate for approximately ten minutes at a time. The preparation would have to be experiential, visual and in a place which would help her to concentrate. Where could we find this material which would help the Rector prepare her?

The Rector and I gathered together a few books and talked to people who had worked with adults who had special needs. From this information we created our own preparation. The core idea was to develop a relationship between Christ and Rachel so that she could receive from that relationship through the celebration of Holy Communion.

Faith Bowers in her book, "Who's This Sitting In My Pew?" (see note below) addressing people with learning difficulties, writes; "We can try and use simple language, we can ensure that there is something in the service in which they can join, but we should not get paranoid about making them understand. Understanding is not our responsibility. We can leave that to God".

We were to start at Rachel's level, meet her where she was in her spirituality, create a flexible structure and leave the understanding to God and Rachel.

Rachel and I frequently prayed in a small Lady Chapel in our church, a place which has serenity and peace. It was there that the Rector decided we should prepare Rachel for her confirmation. The length of each preparation

---

Note: Published by S.P.C.K., Triangle Press.

would be approximately ten minutes and take place each week for twelve weeks.

She knew the "Lord's Prayer" and two choruses. "Father We Adore You" and "Into my Heart". These we decided could be included in each of her preparation classes to form a pattern within the flexible structure.

Relationship was the first experience we wanted to explore with her. In order to avoid confusion it was decided that just Rachel, the Rector and I would gather in the Lady Chapel and I would take a silent rôle, being there to make her feel secure. The Rector began by greeting her by her name and she in her turn greeted the Rector by his Christian name, then they proceeded to have a little chat. The Rector then led Rachel up to the small communion rail and greeted Jesus in a similar way, then they chatted or prayed with Jesus. I knelt a distance away and we ended by saying the "Lord's Prayer". Our Rector had talked to Rachel about Jesus loving her and she stroked his hand.

The preparation continued each week. The Rector introduced a lighted candle to represent Jesus. Rachel felt the warmth from the candle flame as they talked about Jesus's love. She took the candle spontaneously and held it as she stood before the altar and said the Lord's prayer right through. Wonderful.

We introduced the two choruses early on. On some occasions she would not allow me to join in the singing. This was her special time with the Rector and Jesus.

Halfway through Rachel's preparations a very sad yet wonderful event happened. Dorothy, the wife of our minister, John Ducker, who had been so kind and supportive at Rachel's birth, was dying of cancer. I received a letter from John just before one of Rachel's preparation classes, to say that Dorothy only had a few days to live. By now our Rector and Rachel had established, within the confirmation preparation, a time for talking with Jesus. That day our Rector prayed for Dorothy and Rachel repeated every word he said. As he continued to pray, Rachel continued too. The presence of the Holy spirit was so tangible at that moment.

Dorothy died peacefully the following day.

~~~~~ ◊ ~~~~~

Chapter 10

Sharing a Meal with Jesus

Part of our aim in Rachel's confirmation preparation had been achieved, she was beginning to develop a relationship with Jesus. The next part of her preparation was to enable her to receive from Jesus through the Celebration of Holy Communion, a meal the congregation shares with Jesus.

Rachel enjoyed meals, so that is where we started from. We found that we had to be careful not to introduce too many new ideas at a time. Sometimes we made a mistake and Rachel lost concentration. At each preparation we retained the candle as a focal point; a time with the Rector and Rachel talking together in the pews, followed by walking up to the communion rail to talk to Jesus, say the Lord's Prayer, sing the two choruses and finish by sharing the Peace. Where within this structure could we introduce a meal?

We decided to use the time that Rachel and the Rector talked together in the pew. Together they shared marmite sandwiches and looked at photographs of Rachel sharing meals with her friends. Then at the communion rail they both thanked Jesus for friends and shared meals. The following week Rachel looked at pictures of Jesus sharing a meal with his disciples. Afterwards she shared her marmite sandwiches with the Rector. We found some delightful pictures produced in John Vanier's books (see note below), "I meet Jesus" and "I walk with Jesus". The pictures depicted Jesus alongside children with special needs and a priest celebrating communion with similar people. The Rector, using these visual aids, explained how Jesus loves Rachel and how He wants to share a meal with her as an outward show of this love. They then went forward to the communion rail to share the special meal. The Rector showed Rachel how to "cup" her hands to receive the bread and Rachel received with a lovely smile on her face.

Note:- Published by "Little Sisters of Jesus" Anne Sigier Quebec Canada.

That night I went home and wrote these words, "I feel I want to say 'thank you' to all the people who are supporting the Rector, Rachel and me with their prayers. I feel a relationship of love has developed between Jesus and Rachel and Rachel showed this to-day in her joyous response."

Rachel had learnt to receive the bread within an atmosphere of love, with reverence. We decided to introduce the wine in a similar way. First of all with small glasses of orange juice in the pew followed by receiving the wine at the communion rail, within the structure we had already developed. As Rachel received the wine she was taught to say "Amen". She now could say "Amen" in the proper place! This preparation was followed by Rachel receiving the Bread and Wine together, which she did with great reverence. I feel the atmosphere of the Lady Chapel helped. The only conversations that took place in that chapel during Rachel's preparation time were prayers in silence at the beginning and the content of that week's training, nothing else. It became for Rachel a safe and special place where we focused on Jesus and shared a special meal with Him.

Sadly it was our church's custom to use wafers at the celebration of Holy Communion apart from in Family Services. Rachel found this difficult. She would take the wafer, then give it to her Mum. Mum would then eat both her own and Rachel's wafer.

After her final session I wrote this comment at the end of her preparation. "Rachel must have received something special because she seemed so full of peace when she returned home. She didn't play her records as usual but got herself ready for bed. Once in bed she put her hands behind her head and went to sleep with a lovely smile on her face."

I feel that all three of us, the Rector myself and Rachel had received Christ's presence, Christ's love and Christ's peace during the twelve weeks of Rachel's Confirmation Preparation. Christ worked through her to share His abundance of gifts with each of us.

Was this the purpose of Rachel? She received Christ's love so joyously, so spontaneously and then shared His Love with the people she was with. Would this ministry end or develop after she was confirmed?

~~~~~ ◊ ~~~~~

Chapter 11

The Confirmation and After

The thirteenth of November 1988 was the day set aside when Rachel, a number of young people from her peer group and a few adults were to be confirmed at St. Botolph's Church, Aspley Guise. I realised that this would probably be the last time Rachel would take part in an event, which would be the "norm" for her age group. Her mental handicap, especially academically, produced an ever increasing gap between her and her peer group. I realised, too, that she might never be able to earn a living. She would always be dependent, never marry, or produce children. All these thoughts and acknowledgement of what her handicap really meant, made me determined that this confirmation was going to be a special occasion for her and for her family.

We had a very simple cream dress made for her with a large lace collar. A silver cross was given to her to wear. We invited our friends, especially her godparents who had been kind and supportive to us, to come to the service and a celebratory meal afterwards. Our Rector preferred the candidates to be confirmed separately with a sponsor standing beside each of them. I was to be that sponsor, so Rachel wouldn't feel alone. We had a rehearsal for the great day, Rachel responding very well.

The church was packed that Sunday evening, our friends probably having more than Rachel's fair quota of pews! Her headmistress was there, her class teacher, friends from our earlier years and friends from the present. My parents had died during the previous three years. How proud they would have been of Rachel. Both had had a strong Christian Ministry during their lifetimes.

Bishop John Taylor came and sat on a special chair set aside for him and the service began. During his sermon Bishop John made a small reference to handicapped people but in no way was Rachel a focal point. She was a candidate making her commitment to God by being confirmed alongside many others. Because our surname began with "W", we had our usual wait before it was our turn. At last it came. Rachel and I walked up the aisle to the chancel to meet the Bishop and our Rector. Rachel smiled at him and said "Hello", Bishop John smiled back and said, "Hello Rachel". Establishing a relationship had been so much part of the preparation. Rachel knelt down and Bishop John laid his hands on her. Somehow I was aware of only the presence of God, the Rector and the Bishop as Rachel was being confirmed; it felt a bonding of relationship and a receiving of God's Holy Spirit.

The following Sunday, all the confirmation candidates including Rachel were to receive the elements for the first time at a Parish Communion Service. It was a great privilege for John and me to share this receiving from God together with Rachel. She gave me her wafer but looked up to those who ministered to her with great radiance and joy. As she returned to her pew she shared the Peace with various people, as they stood and waited to kneel at the communion rail. A titled member of our congregation later remarked to me, that Rachel had shown him the meaning of the Communion Service. Have we become too academic? Rachel in her simplicity received from God and then shared what she had received.

This continued in a wonderful way. A few months after Rachel had been confirmed, a friend whose father had just died was at the opposite end of the communion rail from Rachel. Suddenly, after she had received the wine, my friend found herself being hugged by Rachel. Another member of our congregation, who was anxious about her son going to the Gulf War, would be hugged by Rachel after she had received communion. Wherever Deirdre sat within the church, Rachel would find her.

What a pity we are all too shy to have Rachel's spontaneity! Surely the warmth of God's love would just flow through our congregations without words, but with just an outward show of affection. Thank you Rachel.

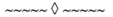

Chapter 12

The Miracle is Broken

Fourteen months after Rachel was confirmed, at the start of 1990 our family circumstances once more had changed. Andrew, our elder son, was in his second year at Warwick University. Martin, our younger son, had left school and was working in a Menswear Department Store in a nearby town. John, my husband, having been made redundant four years earlier, was now permanently at home.

These changes had been stressful and it was difficult to keep depression at bay. Both my husband and I needed counselling to adapt to this new situation. Our sons were marvellous. Both of them became very supportive to and we valued their open relationship with us.

Rachel's needs didn't seem paramount at this time. Apart from the occasional cold she kept well. She appeared to enjoy school, although her progress was very slow.

Every Saturday afternoon Rachel and I went to the Lady Chapel at St. Botolph's Church to pray together, to share bread together and to sing together. I felt the need to do this as Rachel continued not to receive the wafer at the celebration of Holy Communion. I thought that if we continued to share bread together in a place where we could feel God's presence - then hopefully one day in the future, Rachel would receive the bread if it was offered to her at Communion. Anyway it was a very precious time we had together, a time of peace, a time of reflection and a time when we were alone with God.

The weeks went by. The week before Easter, I walked with Rachel to our Village Post Office. Although it was only a short walk it was up and down a steep road. On our return Rachel sat down in the middle of the road. She was blue and having difficulty in breathing. I remembered that a member of staff from school had telephoned the week previously to say that Rachel had been blue and refused to move.

What was I to do? Rachel would not budge. She was panting for breath and we were in the middle of a country road. Fortunately a neighbour came along with his car. We managed to pick Rachel up, put her in the car and take her home.

Next day I took Rachel to our doctor, who after checking her said Rachel's heart murmur had returned and we would need to see a cardiologist.

I felt shattered! Her heart had been healed, it was a miracle! Miracles don't end - they continue! This couldn't happen to Rachel. I was glad that John was at home and our sons were at home for Easter. We were able to support one another. We all loved Rachel so dearly.

I can remember that Good Friday very well. I had been asked to read the part of Mary, Jesus's Mother during the Good Friday service. I was able to enter into her feelings with great understanding. Mary was told before Jesus's birth that her son, God's son, was to be born for a purpose. With this knowledge, how much pain she must have felt that Good Friday as she saw her precious Son being put to death on the cross!

After Easter John and I took Rachel to a number of heart specialists, who seemed hesitant to give us a definite diagnosis. One could hear her murmur, another couldn't. Perhaps it had been a false alarm. But Rachel was becoming increasingly tired, refusing to walk far and having difficulty with the stairs. If I could give a colour to describe that time it would be black. Tension rose within our home because John and I were both anxious.

About the time of Rachel's confirmation I had become interested in Retreats. Turvey Abbey is close to us; a Benedictine Order of Monks and Nuns live here. They organise Guided Retreats, but one can go there to rest and be alone with God, being blessed by the serene atmosphere provided by the Nuns' hospitality.

The Nuns are very keen on creativity. Their beautiful needlework can be seen in many of our churches. Occasionally Retreats are held centred on the creative arts. I went to one of their Day Retreats at the beginning of June 1990. I was feeling low as I walked into one of their houses, Bec House with my various pieces of paper, glues and variety of pens. It was suggested in the silence that we looked around the Abbey Garden for inspiration for Creativity. I went and sat on a small wall, just outside Bec House. I remember how in serene silence, Sister Esther came and sat beside me. Although no words were spoken I could feel her praying for me and I felt held by God's presence.

I smiled. Revived, I looked around me and I noticed a large leafed plant in the small garden in front of me. Within this large leaf was a beautiful pink flower. The large leaf seemed to be enfolding the flower, protecting it.

That is how I felt at that moment in time, enfolded in God's presence and love. I decided to depict this Bergenia Cordifolia in a collage.

I concentrated on the enfolding large leaf with its curves and different colours. I left it for a while to go to Mass and eat my lunch in silence with the other members of the retreat. I felt shut off from humanity, I could relate to the Nuns, I could relate to God, but inside I felt black.

When I returned to the picture I was creating, I studied the large encircling leaf, but in no way could I give that plant a pink flower. I felt black, so black. I produced a black detailed figure. I remember Sister Esther standing behind me as I insisted on that black figure being perfect, enfolded by the leaf. I called this piece of work, my creation from within, "Enfolded in Love".

Three days later we received a letter from Addenbrooke's Hospital, Cambridge. Rachel had an appointment with the Heart Specialist on June 28th 1990.

Chapter 13

Gethsemane

John, Rachel and I walked quite confidently into Addenbrooke's Hospital on that warm June afternoon. We didn't have to wait long before the Heart Consultant saw us. We were led into a room of many machines, surrounded by students. Rachel's heart was scanned - everything showed up in bright colours and the consultant explained the meaning of these colours to the students, but not to us. We were led back to his consulting room, where we sat down and waited. The consultant told us that the hole had returned to Rachel's heart, to the centre of her heart. Most of the energy was being pumped into her lungs but little around the remainder of her body. Nothing could be done - there wasn't any medicine that would help this condition; only a heart and lung transplant would heal her and that was out of the question. Rachel would not survive the operation. We were warned that Rachel would gradually deteriorate, her weight would increase and death might not be too far away; but alternatively Rachel could live for a number of years.

My hopes and my dreams for Rachel just faded away. My husband and I felt stricken. I wanted to sit quietly and let the news sink in, but there was nowhere to go. We left that consulting room stunned, vaguely walking to the Refreshment Room for a cup of tea. All I remember is the clatter of cutlery and all I wanted was peace. All John remembers is my chatter as we drove home. I talked so that I could not be aware of the pain from my feelings. I planned Rachel's room downstairs. We could use John's study, perhaps put a bathroom leading from it somewhere, somehow; could we use the utility room? No - we would need an extension. I was just repeating myself, I had planned Rachel's room at her birth. Practicality or denial on my part? What ever it was, it annoyed John who was feeling the pain of Rachel's diagnosis.

I can't remember much about the following two days. It was strange, I didn't feel the urge to tell people. Rachel was no longer a delightful baby, but rather a plump teenager with problems.

When eventually we began to share our news, I was quite taken aback with some people's reactions. On the whole people thought it would be better if Rachel died, because it would give us more freedom. When our friends had received bad news, I had always sent a small card, but we didn't have any cards come through our letter box. I met with people to pray for those who were ill, but no-one volunteered to pray with us. I was too deep in pain to ask. John became depressed with the pain and more anger from his redundancy came to the surface. Were people once more frightened of my tears or didn't they care? I am sure that they did, but we felt so alone as Christ had done in Gethsemane.

Fortunately our sons had many outside interests by now. They were well weaned from home! I hope our depression and our pain didn't affect them too much.

I remembered my collage that I had created at Turvey a few weeks before we had received Rachel's diagnosis. I placed it in a prominent place in our bedroom. Had God been trying to tell me something through this creative imagery? The large leaf, was that God's enfolding love? What was God trying to tell me? Was it that however black and painful Rachel's diagnosis might be, God was enfolding her with His love? Rachel was precious. God didn't see her as a problem even if humanity did. He would enfold her with His love as He had done since she was born.

In October I returned to Turvey for another day of Creative Art. As it was Autumn we were asked to go out and look for seeds or fallen Autumn leaves. I searched the Abbey Garden and couldn't find anything. Then I had a brilliant idea, or was it God leading me? I returned to the plant Bergenia Cordifolia that I had used for my collage in June. There it was in the garden of Bec House. Everything around it was dead or dying, but I searched within the Bergenia Cordifolia and there to my surprise were new green leaves, new life. I picked some of these new fresh leaves and went back to draw them. It wasn't a magnificent drawing, rather child-like, a new leaf enlarged into a tree. I put red veins flowing through it and called it "New Life". At the end of the session we were asked to explain our Creations. As I spoke, I found myself referring back to the collage I had produced in June, a black figure enfolded by a large leaf. I had now found a new leaf on that same plant and had drawn it with life giving blood. Was Rachel to have a new life? Was it to be in Heaven? Was it to be on earth? It didn't matter to me, the message was that God wanted us to adapt to that new life whatever He chose it to be.

Chapter 14

Reality

"You are like a light for the whole world. A city built on a hill cannot be hidden. No-one lights a lamp and puts it under a bowl; instead he puts it on a lamp stand, where it gives light to everyone in the house". Matthew 5 v14-15.

Prior to writing this chapter I read these words and reflected on the imagery of "New Life" I had created on paper at Turvey Abbey. Rachel had been given to John and me for a purpose. How could we enable God to fulfil his purpose if we sank into the gloom and doom in the abyss of our Gethsemane!

Rachel was still alive, perhaps not the attractive child she once was, but despite being a plump teenager she still had her "Smile of Love" which was so precious to us.

Shortly after my Creative Day at Turvey Abbey, when the seed of "New Life", Rachel's new life, was shown to me, our Rector who had prepared Rachel for her confirmation came to tell us that he and his wife were moving to a new Parish. I was saddened at the news, because he and his wife were a great support to us. Our Rector was a man of prayer. If we had to give new life to Rachel and come face to face with the reality of her deteriorating condition, we were not to wait until someone volunteered to pray with us. Our Rector would soon be leaving.

The following Thursday, as I left church after attending morning Communion, a voice within me said, "Ask and it shall be given unto you". I returned to the church door but I just hadn't the courage to go back into the church to ask the Rector to pray with John and me. I walked further down the road, past Miss Watson sitting on the seat outside the Rectory; again from within me I heard, "Ask and it shall be given unto you". I returned to the church and actually entered into the porch, but no - I couldn't ask! Once more I passed Miss Watson sitting on the seat as I walked further down the road, only to hear that voice more loudly within me "Ask and it shall be given unto you!" Miss Watson looked at me very strangely as I passed her once more sitting on that public bench! This time I went into the church, up the aisle and into the Rector's Vestry. It wasn't difficult to ask. I told him how John and I couldn't adapt to Rachel's situation, and asked if he could please come and pray with us before he left the parish.

The Rector came on four occasions to pray with us before he left the parish. We had the courage to give all our problems out aloud to God. On our final meeting there was a very strong presence of the Holy Spirit with us.

Slowly John and I began to see a light in the darkness of that abyss. Praying together gave us the strength to adapt to the reality of Rachel's situation.

On a practical level we had to bring Rachel downstairs. The thoughts and plans I had talked about on our way home from Addenbrooke's Hospital, now came in useful. John used a long narrow room next door to our cloakroom as a study. John moved the contents of that room into a vacant bedroom upstairs. We added a bay window to the narrow room, put down a green carpet, hung up some beautiful curtains with a pelmet, plus some corner wardrobes, mounted a television on the wall, added a dressing table and "Hey Presto" Rachel had a bed-sitting room!. It didn't happen overnight. We had to plan and save money for it, but it was a focus for us - also an outward show of Rachel leaving her childhood and having an adult bed-sitting room of her own.

Two of the ways in which Rachel's deterioration was manifesting itself were her increasing weight and incontinence. They needed to be addressed, but how? As her eighteenth birthday drew near, we realised that we needed a downstairs bathroom. When her brothers had reached their eighteenth birthdays, Andrew had proceeded to University to enable him to study for a career. Martin had received financial help with a car to enable him to travel to work. Rachel needed something to enable her to have a better quality of life. A small jacuzzi? Her bed sitting room backed on to our utility room. We took a third off the latter, put a door in her room leading to a very small corner-shaped jacuzzi. It has been well worth the expense. The jacuzzi relaxes her and the moving water stimulates her circulation. We can bathe her regularly without too much strain on ourselves and within an even temperature. Rachel has kept remarkably healthy, only having a few colds. I just rejoice that John and I were able to save the money for these alterations. It gave us great delight to see our plans become reality and despite the gloomy diagnosis, Rachel still has a good quality of life.

We have received help with her diet and we just about manage to keep her weight stable, but Rachel likes her food!

When we came to live close to Milton Keynes, we thought it was because of John's company moving to this area, but John was made redundant. Our sons certainly benefited from the move. The greatest aspect of all though is that Milton Keynes is flat. It is built to accommodate wheelchairs with its Redways and undercover Shopping Centre. Rachel is now in a wheelchair, but living here doesn't stop us from taking her for walks exploring the City Centre and parking is so easy.

From my experience of God I have come to believe that He is there before us, preparing a way. He has really provided for all Rachel's needs. Forgive me God when I become anxious and forget to have faith and trust in You.

~~~~~ ◊ ~~~~~

Chapter 15

Rachel's Ministry

Before Rachel was born, I thought that God's ministry was only carried out by clergy, pastors and missionaries. A friend who gave us support during the first few years of Rachel's life said to me before she moved to another town that she would probably forget many of the sermons she had heard, but she would never forget Rachel and her love. That statement made me think; Rachel has little language, how could she have a ministry that was remembered above that of clergy? It is a different kind of ministry.

It is a ministry of love, of sensitivity, of weakness and of her wonderful smile especially when she receives communion. It is a facilitating ministry that enables people to share their deepest feelings whatever their status. John and I have become safe people to share with, because when people see us with Rachel they know we have been through pain, disappointment and rejection. John and I have both been drawn towards counselling and befriending because Rachel has given us a greater sensitivity towards people.

No longer do I have the status or the salary of a teacher. I had planned to return to my profession once my children needed less mothering. It's been hard for me to shed that status but in other ways my life has been richer, not in a commercial sense, but because of the experiences Rachel has enabled me to have. The fellowship of other parents who have handicapped children is fulfilling. We all share a common bond what ever our status may be. Together we have formed support groups so that our children can have a better quality of life.

It is the outward expression of Rachel's love that has impressed me.

Through her God has enabled me to acknowledge the gifts he has given to me and to put into perspective those gifts which I have inherited. Despite being shy, I have the gift of performance. I automatically thought that I had to use this gift in order to loved, to be a Christian! It was my aim in life to be "up front" to be honoured and admired. God has taught me many a painful lesson through Rachel, that he loves me just as I am! He can use my shyness and my gentleness much more than my performance. Recently I have "let go" of all my rôles that involved any kind of performance. This took me through a wilderness period from which I emerged with more confidence in the knowledge that God wanted me to share His love through Rachel.

When I was a child I enjoyed writing poetry, a gift which lay dormant for many years. This gift manifested itself in the abyss of our Gethsemane. Often in my spiritual journal I would write pages about my pain, then condense these words into a poem, small enough to focus on, small enough to hand over to God to be healed.

Later when John and I were seeing the light within our abyss we were able to go to a Personality and Prayer Retreat at Turvey, whilst Rachel was in Respite Care. We were asked to write a poem based on the 23rd Psalm. Who was our Shepherd? In an amazingly short time I wrote the following:-

> The Lord is my handicapped daughter, Rachel.
> She lets me rest within her arms
> And leads me into her peace.
> Her gentleness, her warmth and her smile of love
> Revive me, and take away my fear.
> As we travel on our journey together
> As she gradually deteriorates
> Her ministry of love is always with me.
> Wherever her presence is, has been or will be
> The pain, the joy and the love of
> Rachel will always remain.

This piece of prose or poetry was later broadcast on Radio Four and is now included in Rosemary Hartill's book "Were You There" (Note at bottom of this page)

What a wonderful ministry our daughter has been given, little language, unable to walk far, incontinent, of extremely low intelligence, yet God is using her to minister His love in a very wonderful way.

~~~~~ ◊ ~~~~~

Note: Published by S.P.C.K. January 1995

Chapter 16

Conclusion

Has Rachel been born for a purpose? She has certainly changed the lives of John and myself and has brought us closer to God.

As parents, we have been influenced by Rachel to accept all our children, Andrew, Martin and Rachel herself, as they are, and not as we feel they ought to be. We began to realise that academic achievement was not to be our main focus in our parenting. Rachel's personality needed to develop from the gifts God had given her, a beautiful smile, her gentleness, her sensitivity. This realisation helped us to be aware of our sons' individual potentials and encourage them to develop. We have made some mistakes! John and I also learned about the importance of commendation and not condemnation in our attitude towards our children.

Rachel has had an influence on all three church families we have belonged to. We have now moved on to the Ecumenical Church of Christ the Cornerstone in Milton Keynes. On a practical level it is more accommodating for disabled people. We wanted Rachel to participate completely in receiving both the elements at Holy Communion. Because of the acceptance of the many disabled people within this Church Family, I think that Rachel feels a member of it. It was a great joy to John and me when Rachel received both the bread and the wine at the Lord's Table in Christ the Cornerstone and she has continued to do so.

Our main focus at St. Botolph's was Rachel's confirmation and her simplicity of receiving that influences many people. We still pray together in the Lady Chapel and I know that many people within this congregation pray for Rachel. We value these prayers.

Within our beloved little Methodist Church in West Horsley, whose minister in our time there, John Ducker died on March 24th 1995, Rachel's presence drew out so much love and support, which gave John and me foundations at the beginning of our family life with Rachel.

Within the larger community, Rachel has given us the courage to insist that people with special needs are individuals who need a good quality of life, who have needs which need to be met. I hope that by joining Support Groups and initiating others we have played a small part in the acceptance of mentally handicapped people into the community.

There is still much to be done. The most painful part of having a handicapped daughter for John and me is the isolation and rejection from society, which increases as Rachel grows older. I have not dwelt too much on this aspect within this book, because I wanted it to show what can happen when Rachel is positively accepted.

What has it meant to me personally having Rachel as a daughter? Without a doubt it has brought me closer to God. Having a handicapped child brings you time and time again down to rock bottom, whatever your status. My trust and faith in God is paramount. I share everything with Him - humanity soon becomes bored, quite naturally, with my pain, my anxiety and rejection. But God doesn't, He listens continually and eventually a peace between us materialises. Within that peace a voice always tells me that God wouldn't have given me Rachel unless He went before her, preparing places and people who will accept and nurture her.

Our journey and our experience with Rachel has led me to a greater understanding of Christ's Ministry on earth. Christ met people where they were and listened to them with love and compassion. We have had to meet Rachel where her potential is and to relate to the Christ within her. I am gradually learning to relate to the Christ within the people I meet. God accepts us as we are, but He doesn't always like the things we do! I have shared a little in His Gethsemane, in His rejection, in the darkness of His abyss. We have rejoiced in Resurrection experiences. Each simple achievement which Rachel produces is a joy - a celebration.

But above all it is her love that has had the greatest influence upon my life. I can only express this emotion as a poem which I wrote after Rachel had received both elements at the Lord's Table at Christ the Cornerstone, Milton Keynes on April 10th 1994.

To-day we were fed
Rachel and I
With bread and wine

The people who
Fed us, Lord,
Were kind
Were gentle
Filled with your love.

The bread, Your body,
Broke in Rachel's hand.
It didn't matter, Lord.
I picked up the piece
The broken piece
And fed her, Lord.

The wine, Your blood,
Was given to her
Gently, sensitively.
The man bent down
And met her where she was
Small vulnerable, Lord,
But filled with Your love.

She was led back to her seat
Gently, kindly by a friend
Who too is broken.
He held her hand
And guided her.

Oh Lord I cried
That this love
Your love
Was given and received
By Rachel, enfolded in love.

Has Rachel been born for a purpose?
I leave that answer to you, reader of this book.

~~~~~ ◊ ~~~~~